The New Economy

Also by Gabrielle Calvocoressi

Rocket Fantastic

Apocalyptic Swing

The Last Time I Saw Amelia Earhart

The New Economy

Gabrielle Calvocoressi

COPPER CANYON PRESS
PORT TOWNSEND, WASHINGTON

Printed in the United States of America

Cover art: Courtesy of Centrum. Photo by Kevin Elliff.

Copper Canyon Press is in residence at Fort Worden State Park in Port Townsend, Washington, under the auspices of Centrum. Centrum is a gathering place for artists and creative thinkers from around the world, students of all ages and backgrounds, and audiences seeking extraordinary cultural enrichment.

LIBRARY OF CONGRESS CATALOGING-IN-PUBLICATION DATA
Names: Calvocoressi, Gabrielle author
Title: The new economy / Gabrielle Calvocoressi.
Description: Port Townsend, Washington : Copper Canyon Press, 2025. |
Summary: "A collection of poems by Gabrielle Calvocoressi"— Provided by publisher.
Identifiers: LCCN 2025022882 (print) | LCCN 2025022883 (ebook) |
ISBN 9781556597213 hardcover | ISBN 9781619323186 epub
Subjects: LCGFT: Poetry
Classification: LCC PS3603.A4465 N49 2025 (print) |
LCC PS3603.A4465 (ebook) | DDC 811/.6—dc23/eng/20250613
LC record available at https://lccn.loc.gov/2025022882
LC ebook record available at https://lccn.loc.gov/2025022883

9 8 7 6 5 4 3 2

COPPER CANYON PRESS
Post Office Box 271
Port Townsend, Washington 98368
www.coppercanyonpress.org

To Randall Kenan, Lucie Brock-Broido,
and Jenny Tone-Pah-Hote

Miss you

Contents

Lent Cisterns: Could I Ever Write a Poem Again After These Years of Bleeding These Years of Mourning?

The New Economy

Hammond B-3 Organ Cistern

The days I don't want to kill myself
are extraordinary. Deep bass. All the people
in the streets waiting for their high fives
and leaping, I mean *leaping*
when they see me. I am the sun-filled
god of love. Or at least an optimistic
undersecretary. There should be a word for it.
The days you wake up and do not want
to slit your throat. Money in the bank.
Enough for an iced green tea every weekday
and Saturday and Sunday! It's like being
in the armpit of a Hammond B-3 organ.
Just reeks of gratitude and funk.
The funk of ages. *I am not going to ruin*
my love's life today. It's like the time I said yes
to gray sneakers but then the salesman said
Wait. And there, out of the back room,
like the bakery's first biscuits: bright blue kicks.
Iridescent. Like a scarab! Oh who am I kidding
it was nothing like a scarab! It was like
bright. blue. fucking. sneakers! I did not
want to die that day. Oh my god.
Why don't we talk about it? How good it feels.
And if you don't know then you're lucky
but also you poor thing. Bring the band out on the stoop.
Let the whole neighborhood hear. Come on, Everybody.
Say it with me nice and slow
          no pills   *no cliff*   *no brains on the floor*
Bring the bass back.   *no rope*   *no hose*   not today, Satan.
Every day I wake up with my good fortune
and news of my demise. Don't keep it from me.

Why don't we have a name for it?
Bring the bass back. Bring the band out on the stoop.
Hallelujah!

Affirmation Cistern When I Let Go of My Fear My Life Becomes Magical

The trees and I open our mouths
together and become a different
kind of vessel. A lightship full of birdsong.
On my back in the grass, floating.
The trees show me their God face,
which are more faces than I can count.
I open all the holes in me so I become
a saxophone or a viola da gamba.
Whichever I feel. It's good
to open for the trees, who don't
force me. We make a loop of music
and I let the river in as well.
It's almost too much but I can stop
whenever I want to. That's how kind
the trees are. How respectful.

What I can't remember is
how my light body got stolen.
Or why the bed spun every
night. And why I couldn't
move. Sometimes, the trees
say, it's best to speak plainly.
I'm trying, I say. I'm really trying.

I Was Supposed To Cistern: Redbud Variation

Book a hotel room but I looked
out my window instead   little act of resistance

that let me see the redbud was about to bloom.

I was supposed to think about my president
                                        and all the wars   all the bodies

all the tanks rolling into all the cities   I was supposed to

                                        have my eye to the ground.

Children piled beneath the empty cisterns. Eyes hollowed out by vultures
to get to the meatiest part,

                            which are the memories

                                        willful and resilient in the
                                        spongy folds.

                        What a terrible friend and citizen I was
that morning.

          I did know the tanks were rolling over the bodies.

          I did know I'd help poison over half of the world.

          Choke hold on the bashful scrotum.
          Sixty hours of blasting Megadeth
          in the throbbing cell.

Miss you. Would like to take a walk with you.

Do not care if you arrive in just your skeleton.
Would love to take a walk with you. Miss you.
Would love to make you shrimp saganaki.
Like you used to make me when you were alive.
Love to feed you. Sit over steaming
bowls of pilaf. Little roasted tomatoes
covered in pepper and nutmeg. Miss you.
Would love to walk to the post office with you.
Bring the ghost dog. We'll walk past the waterfall
and you can tell me about the after.
Wish you. Wish you would come back for a while.
Don't even need to bring your skin sack. I'll know
you. I know you will know me even though. I'm
bigger now. Grayer. I'll show you my garden.
I'd like to hop in the leaf pile you raked but if you
want to jump in? I'll rake it for you. Miss you
standing looking out at the river with your rake
in your hand. Miss you in your puffy blue jacket.
They're hip now. I can bring you a new one
if you'll only come by. Know I told you
it was okay to go. Know I told you it was okay
to leave me. Why'd you believe me?
You always believed me. Wish you would
come back so we could talk about truth.
Miss you. Wish you would walk through my
door. Stare out from the mirror. Come through
the pipes.

Inheritance Cistern Sweet Dominion

They had their lightning thrones, they had
their cages. They had their lamb pens and lamb
ties not just for lambs but for their own. As soon
as I understood the name of my skin sack
I was handed the chain. Was told by virtue
of my snow-lit skin I was Courtier
of the Chain. And could be Lord Chancellor
if I played my cards right. *Dominion.* We worked
the word over and over. We practiced with butterscotch
and Jolly Ranchers in the gold Honda. In the mile-long
yellow chariot that ferried us to the Coliseum.
So sweet. No need to bite down for the whole world
to hear you. No need to work your jaws
like an animal. To make yourself into an animal.

But also. Useful to think like an animal. To know
what that smelled like. That fear. My little skin
sack and really such a weakling who wept
over the stupidest things. Particularly
when waiting for the long yellow chariot.
I want to go home. To where? That was the rub.
No more home for me. If there ever was one.
I pitied myself. Little skin sack with the young wolves
circling in their gladiator suits. Heart refusing
to harden. But. The taste of hatred ::

the sweet promise of that possible release.
In the annals of my light scroll when and if the
light takes me back, it will be impossible to deny.
After the kicks and taunts. After hours eating
Salisbury steak over the toilet in the girls'
restroom. After the turnaway the plague

game, bags of piss and shit thrown from passing
chariots as I made my way to the fairgrounds
on foot? They made a wager and let a lamb sack out
before me. And battered it. And battered it.
But all the while looking at me. Who laughed
along with them. My relief inexhaustible

as my desolation the next day when, having
shown myself to lamb and wolf entirely,
I was given my true calling. Which was exile
from every realm.

Karma Affirmation Cistern Don't Be Afraid Keep Going Toward the Horror

Remember how you didn't fall yesterday
even though you thought you would?
Life can be like that all the time if you
let it. Remember all the balance beams
and the room full of stuffed animals
at the children's hospital. How scary it
was and always dark? It was meant
to be comforting but you knew better
and survived it. That gauntlet of stuffed
animals leading to the physical therapy room.
So long ago. When you learned it's okay
to hold out your hand and help someone up.
No matter what the factory or the nurses
tell you. A good thing to remember is that life
is an equal amount of doughnut shops
and roadkill every day. And if you see
the deer get hit you can call the tiger
rescue group and the deer will become
tiger food. Sometimes the things
that matter to you won't matter
to anyone but you. And that's redemption.
The poem that means nothing to anyone
but you. Like how your life was.
Like your bones that you kept safe
and the meatloaf you hid in the corner
of your mouth so it wouldn't get stolen
off your plate. It is true that sometimes
you want to take the food off other people's
plates. Let that sink in and then remember
it's okay. To know you're part craven smuggler.
Part thief. Maybe if you know your animal.

I mean really know your animal.
You won't become a builder of factories
or slave ships. Maybe instead of building
a ship somewhere in your body
you just let yourself feel the pain and
humiliation. No need to make it beautiful
for some future reader. Just say how much
you wanted to hurt someone like you got hurt.
And then just watch that for a while. It's okay
to feel horribly ashamed. Best not to look away.
The gate to joy is past the factory and past
the reader and maybe it's past your last breath
on this planet. There's nothing you can do about it.
You come from the cistern of brutality
and hunger. You are the resonator. Just breathe.

Light Body Cistern Be Gone from the Place You Almost Destroyed

All our light bodies came to the party
gleaming. We let down our furs and suits
of armor. We glistened. *Glistened.* We were
light as the transparencies our teachers
used in school. Our brightness lit the river
landing. Not a single light was needed
in the houses. We were the light. The boats
arriving one by one. We burned them. With our light
bodies. Ship back to pine into ash. We wept.
We let the howl out. We grieved our hunger
for the forests, for the lands, for the bodies,
for the bodies, for the bodies. We set out
for the factory. One long procession of light.
We pulled the blood from the ground
as we walked. With our light bodies.
And it seemed a lifetime ago. When we had
bathed ourselves in blood of everything
we'd made weaker than us. When we'd
reveled in the blood. We burned
the money with our light bodies. Why
had we wanted it so much? Days waiting
underground, the smell of piss and shit
surrounding us. People jumping on the tracks
and us still making our dogged way to work.
Sometimes we'd fall on our knees from
the sorrow of what we'd done. On our way
to the factory. But that too was a mercy
now. Let free of the skin that we refused
to call *pink.* The church stared back at us.
White even in the darkness that covered
everything. Built from the forests that used
to surround our little towns, our vast cities.

Slashed. We stripped the sky of birdsong.
All the birds returning now to watch us make
our way. They filled the space behind us
as if we'd never been there. Remarkable.
The land didn't miss us at all. Somewhere
the sound of bears letting their shoulders
relax. The bucks' racks clattering behind
us, overjoyed and bounding into each other
at the news of our leaving. We howled
and the wolves howled with us. But they
were full of joy. And we were meant
to finally know the horror. In our light
bodies. But that too was a mercy. One
we certainly didn't deserve. After so much
blood. So many bodies beneath our feet,
our forearms, trailing behind the back
of our pickup trucks. Oh, how we loved
to drag them behind our chariots. And before us
a wall of stallions formed. No passage through
until we'd named them. Every single one.
The bodies. Days turned into years turned into
the light sucked from us. Back to the stars
that deserved it. And the horses with their
heads bowed. Their ponies holding them back
from charging. *Go,* they finally said.
And would not meet the place our eyes had been.
Oh. To be hated by the animals. We felt it now.
The earth's disgust. How had we thought
we were divinity? That we deserved
everything. Where were the others?
We looked around and saw we were alone.
In our light bodies. Brightness we'd wanted
so badly we refused the sow, the coral,
the cherry blossom, the sweet cream we could

have made our name from. Now nothing
but the stark white light of our loneliness.
Even at the end we wanted pity and recognition.
But everyone else was busy rebuilding
and rejoicing. We could smell the grass behind us.
Little sprigs bursting forth. Free of us.

Reawakening Cistern: Recovering the Golden Thread

Sometimes I get so deep inside the music
I can't get myself out. What my teacher calls
fantasizing I call deeper in the golden cistern.
Lush cavity of the burl I watch for hours with
my headphones on. Playing Laraaji and wondering
about all the people who think you need
to talk about the present to write a poem.
In the present I am writing a poem where
I go back into my light body. Because
what's so interesting about saying last night
I made a supper so disgusting I can't
even face throwing it out today? I do that.
I get overly ambitious and before I know
it what was meant to be a feast has turned
into a disappointment. What's the point
of belaboring it? I thought the rice would
cook in forty-five minutes if I boiled it in
the curry. I was wrong. Is this the stuff
of poems? All day I imagined the golden
thread rebraiding between me and my
planet. I could get so deep into the green,
could hear the rivers meeting, could see
my grandmother just about to push the portal
open and bring out plates for supper
so we could eat on the patio. Heaven
is something I'm aspiring to. I try to make
it here on Earth. For years people told
me I couldn't write a poem worth reading.
Couldn't think a thought worth discussing.
Couldn't feed the dog right. Couldn't walk.
Couldn't make a body like the other beings
made a body. One day I walked away from

the empire of the expertise of others.
This is the part in the song where the Moog
gets so aggressive. Well. That's one way
to look at it. The other way is it's pouring
light into the place my heart is meant to be.

Light Body Cistern Eyehole Pendulum Return

Slipping everywhere. My eyeholes aching
in the mornings, making it impossible to eat

my eggs and bacon. I knew it wasn't a tragedy.
And if I swung my head back and forth

I could fix it. It felt so good. Back and forth
and the light slipping in and out around me.

I was a ring of light around my skin sack.
What I heard them call a halo in the God house.

Back and forth and then I was inside it, the nausea
became . . . luminous. At the market. At the table.

At the God house. Swinging myself whole. Until the men
who heal the bodies said, *Stop. We don't swing*

our heads back and forth out here. The mysteries
of this planet. Unaccountable. But I stopped. Or. Went into

my bedroom to just be in my light body. Placed my eyes
gently on the white covers, so just the blue buds were visible.

Poor things, I'd whisper to them. Let them rest
as I unfurled myself into every corner of the room.

Maternal Cistern Long Cold Lonely Winter Little Walk

Wake up, little light body, she whispered
in my ear. It took nothing. I'd been waiting
for her to ask to see me.

Over I turned and flung
the blankets back. Here I am! Little light
body ready to go.

Wishing she would show me hers, I shone
a little brighter. Showed her how my heart
portal blazed green and blue,

how much faster I could
walk when it was just my light body. Without
my stupid eyes. Even now. Before sunrise.

How I wanted to please her. All the chariots
lazy by their ranches. Look at us!
Running. Well. Me running. Her blazing

the trail ahead. Warrior.

So cool. Walking through the darkness.
Just us. I could feel my light body thrumming
with joy. No. It was her. Singing!

And also making a sound like a wolf. And also a sound like a whale.
Sort of scary. But. Also, here we were. Together. Just us.

Wait up! My light body racing to meet her.
Not even in shoes. Not even in her robe.
Just her thin pajamas. Walking so fast. Holy moly.

Penal Cistern Lightning Throne

My skin sack was taken to the Hall of Pictures
in the Capitol. My Zips seemed made
to slide across the marble floor. Though
careful careful of my balance. So walked
slow as the other kids flew by. Slow
and serious skater. Past the paintings
and the statues of steel men in bowler
hats. Past the light bodies of young men
reaching, naked, snake bodies curled
around their calves. I paused to lay
my hands and forehead on and was told
Stop. A lake in the floor. A *cistern.*
We filled it with pennies, which were
wishes. Just one though. Not to be
greedy. Just one wish for myself I was
told.

All the way through the white
halls to where the rooms opened out.
And at the far end, alone on the wall,
black and white, like a newspaper
photo on a canvas: a throne powered
by lightning. Leather belts
like my father wore to work. But thicker.
And for the wrists and forehead.
At the center of the throne: a strap
like our bus driver unhooked
when he'd pull the yellow chariot over
to separate the young gladiators
huddled over me. *So the body doesn't bolt.*
And on top, a shining mixing bowl, welcome
side down. Which we were told was the crown

that held the lightning in.

Penal Cistern Lightning Throne Lightning Rebounded

Back into the body all the lightning goes
back into the body. Up through the crown
of the skull and round again like the Whip ride
at the fairgrounds. Pushing the boundaries
of the light body. Overloading the light
body. Silly bowl shaking above the bowl
of the skull, which is a bowl holding court over
bowl the brain. Bowl into bowl into bowl.
All the curves pressing together. Too much
light in the light body. Body of cattle after long

days of sweet grasses, after chariot ride and hug
tunnel that opens to the bolt to the head.
After, the hook swinging the skin sack through
the air to the place they release the skin.
Skin ferried to the shop in Missouri or North
Carolina to be stretched, tanned, and cut
into strips that make the belts that hold the arms
down, the ankles back, the head steady.
So the crown may grace the head of those

who fight against its glory.

Snow Day Cistern

The snow cloaked the redbud
with its whiteness and didn't
make a big deal about it. Didn't

crush the redbud or suck up
all the oxygen. I watched for a long
time. In my office trying to make

some ideas go together. My eyes
hurt a lot and I thought, *Just look wide.*
Tried to sit with the blurriness

and nausea. Flakes reeling outside
covered the car. *Blanket,*
is what I thought. The weather

vessel said it wouldn't last for long.

Homecoming Cistern Alien Vessel

Oh, my planet, how beautiful
you are. Little curve that leads me
to the lakeside. Let me step out

of the sack of skin I wore
on Earth. It's good to be home.
No more need to name me. No more

need to make the shape of a machete
with my mouth. Pushing up up up the tired
sides that want to drop below my teeth.

Lord, I've missed you. The streets
covered all day in light from the moons.
I was confused all the time. I wanted so much.

My hole felt like a gut with an antler
rammed through it. So lonely and strange
and always trying to smile. Coin of the realm.

And my arms open and my life
coming in and out of the "ATM."
Once I saw a fox leap inside the morning

light and made the same shape
of myself. Once I watched the boats
and also rocked back and forth.

How does every person not cry out
all the time? Yes, it was good to eat
doughnuts. Yes. I was blessed by many

days of joy. A rabbit in the driveway.
A rosemary bush with a sorcerer's cloak
of spiderwebs. Brian Eno.

The Hammond B-3 organ that never asked
me who I knew. But that body.
Like a factory. That mind like a ship

built to pile in other bodies. Skin like a
sow without any of the sow's equanimity.
It reflected nothing. Pink skin. Blue eyes

hard as an anvil. Like a window with covering
that refuses the passerby's gaze. I loved
the bully power some days. Oh my pleasure

in *not* causing harm. My pride. I'm not like
so-and-so. My pink skin preaching, my pink skin
yawping out my other hole, "I did not choke

the man with my elbow!" "Would never!"
"I let *all* the boys in hoodies walk
through dark streets." "I did not shoot

them with my guns!" The ship rising
up inside me. As if the fox felt pride
for not tearing the bird to pieces. As if

the owl's heart grew large from not
wrecking the squirrel's nest. My pink skin
a sail full of indignation. My eyes pitching

across the feed. It is so good to be home
and yet. I have a ship inside. How can
the organ welcome me? I'm not a sow

on her worst day. Which would be what?
Breaking from the barn? Eating all the acorns
and rolling in the mud? No.

Her worst would be at my hands
and on my plate for supper. *Grow*
like the tree, the man who heals

the bodies said. In every way I became
the ship rising in the harbor.
How can I be welcomed after that?

Miss you. Would like to grab that chilled tofu that we love.

Do not care if you only bring your light body.
Would just be so happy to sit at the table
and talk about the menu. Miss you.
Wish we could bet which chilies they'll put
on the cubes of tofu. Our favorite.
Sometimes green. Sometimes red. Roasted
we always thought. But so cold and fresh.
How did they do it? Wish you could be here
to talk about it like it was so important.
Wish you could. Watched you on the screens
as I was walking as I was cooking. Wished you
could get out of the hospital. Can't
bring myself to order our dish and eat it
in the car. Miss you laughing. Miss
you coming in from the cold and one
too many meetings. Laughing. I'll order
already. I'll order seven helpings some
dumplings those cold yam noodles that you
like. You can come in your light
body or skeleton or be invisible I don't even
care. Know you have a long way to travel.
Know I don't even know whether it's long
at all. Wish you could tell me. What
you're reading. If you're reading.
Miss you. I'm at the table in the back.

What When the Ancestors Turn from Us

Not angrylike, no. Not fire and brimstone.
Not the sugar bowl rattling the windows
flying open slamming shut. Not some skeleton
train hurtling through the dining room. Not rude.
The Italian poet said what I really needed
was to *understand when to break the line.*
Not that: condescension ripe as a liverwurst
factory on fire. Maybe the *what what what*
choppers flying low over neighborhood
hour after hour. Not. Searchlights wakeful
they snake through our houses looking for. What?
When the ancestors turn from us they just
won't come at all. Or fly past our spaghetti arms
at the bus stop winded running behind.

Mayflower Cistern I Feel My Pilgrim Worry

All day long I feel my pilgrim
worry. Crude and unforgiving
as the buckle on my boots. I mark
the boundaries of the town
and then, I build a fence. I build
a pillory and scaffold. I bring
my gun into the forests.
And my axe. Inside me. I hurl
my brittle body at the pines.
I have a plan for them. A way
to make them useful, which
is God's compact with the world.
Whatever does not welcome
me I tear asunder. Whatever
welcomes me was mine to
sack and bring to my knees.
I give the gift of my hunger
to everyone. And then
I build a fence. The doe
is certainly a sorceress.
The sparrow was the woman
smiling into the mirror
of the well. What will I make
of this country? Inside me.
My pilgrim huddles in the corner
of my heart. Which I hate
for its hopeful sounding.
Its unwillingness to know
the truth of how broken
and beyond salvation it is.

Neighbor Reckoner Cistern Michael Comes to Help

Your face at the door, Michael! I put my mask on
you see me through the window and pull up
your gaiter! Now we speak with our eyes.
Shining! Yesterday you were crying but today
we're walking to the backyard with the sun
pouring all over our light bodies. I feel my
breath through my mask. What does it mean
to have work for you? Rid of credit and the factory
I grew up in. The light pours over
us. You say, *Do you have a belt? It's going*
to get annoying. Pulling your pants up
for emphasis. Michael, I wish I had a body
like yours. I've dreamed of a body like yours.
Adorning my light body. Not so tall. Muscular.
My whole life I've wanted my shirt to fit
the way yours does. Do I have a belt? You
bet I do. It fits you fine because yours is
the kind of waist I've dreamed of. We're laughing.
You wear it better than I do! I say with wonder
instead of jealousy. Why do I only feel
wonder instead of jealousy when it comes
to bodies? But jealousy like a shot
of hot sauce on an oyster when it comes
to money and success. The leaves fall
around us. *I can only pay so much,*
I say. It stretches the word *neighbor* so it
groans a little bit. I remember hearing
if you play Bach on period instruments
you can hear the wood pushing to the edge
of its possibility. Are we like that? Viola da
gamba shuddering in the concert hall.
All of us shuddering with it. Yesterday

you were crying and I sent you away
saying, *Come back tomorrow I'll have*
money. Tomorrow. I could have offered
you a meal. I had pot roast in the fridge.
When you were late in coming
I worried and kicked myself. What could
have kept you safe if you were in trouble?
Me. That's who. Neighbor. We stand
in the sunlight: you: the body I dream of: and me:

The Year I Didn't Kill Myself Cistern

Is this year, so far. Though I think
about it to self-soothe. Which is an
admission and also admonition
because sometimes I tell myself
to stop. Self-immolation and vengeance
get me through most days and dark
nights when praying for everyone's
safety doesn't seem to help. Dark
tunnel of the self, I wandered
lonely as a cloud and no one
texted or called to see that I was
okay. That day. But most days,
oh wait, I've written that poem
before. I walk out to the beehive
we host but don't own. And
watch them form their writhing
beard. Sometimes they fly around
me. Sometimes they make a pleasant
drone. One time I watched a neighbor
hive pull the bees out and kill
them, drag them, piles of them
on the ground and a stardust
of wax covering them like a blanket
or glitter from a party downtown.
They'd come and bashed the shit
out of the comb as they stole
all the nectar, made waste of all
that labor our furred neighbors
had done. I'd walk out and watch
them make their way in and out
of the box, four gallons of honey
for my cup and many more gallons

left inside to keep them fed for
the winter. All gone. No one
who doesn't have bees can believe
it. How vicious the season can be.
How every being will slaughter
their neighbor if they're hungry
and   enough.

Bringing the bees

To the back corner

the hive the vessel the box where the bees live

Chris says,   They need a runway

They need to know what's their space

You can have a small space and it's fine as long as they have their space

I'm torn because I couldn't really open   Not even under anesthesia?

No

So I'm torn   torn and waiting   to hear what's buzzing inside me

I say to myself: It's just your heart buzzing   it's just your brain

But I don't know   My teacher had us imagine we had

Seven years to live

Seven months to live

Seven weeks to live

Seven days

Seven hours

I spent the whole seven seconds just counting

Michael When You Left I Heard Three Shots

It's weird how much when I was little I wanted
to be tough to beat people up to own a gun.
Wanted the boy body that would keep my body
from being so scared. Michael, when you
left I heard three quick shots. What people
visiting insist are firecrackers but are most certainly
not. I wanted to beat people up in broad
daylight. I wanted to make grown men beg
for their lives. It helped me go to sleep to imagine
it. My body huge with muscles. My eyes hard
and never sorry. Vengeance a mandala. Vengeance
a gauntlet covering my light body. I let it
pour over me and harden as I drifted to sleep.

Nobility Cistern We Have Stalwart Friend

There were more dark corridors
on this planet that I could fathom.
Everywhere, a dark corridor. In the
houses for sleep and the houses for
healing. In the God houses. In the
skin houses that cooed and bludgeoned
and sometimes both at once. So many
dark places. And always something
coming to find you when you just
wanted some privacy. Even the dinner
plate had its dark corners. So even
my food wasn't my own. Where
did it come from? The arm and then
darkness and all my chicken casserole
and vegetables gone.

You could get killed for not passing
the salt. You could get killed for not
saying good morning. You could get
every bone in your body broken
because you didn't bring in the paper,
didn't keep the woodstove burning,
didn't get the ball in the basket. No.
It was a joke. I was supposed to be
laughing.

A good way to know was how they
treated their animals. I lay awake
in my light body and heard the wooden
pointer whistling through the air
until it hobbled the dog. Into my light body:
her light body whimpering. Cowered.

But then licking the forearm. Then running
along the riverbanks beside it.

Sometimes I'd hit the dog too. With the newspaper
rolled tight into a log. Hollow. Hollow drum of her flank.

My head hung with her forehead resting on mine.

Stacking Cistern My Bones on Top of Your Bones on Top of Your Bones

Not an optimist. I lie awake at night and say the name
of everyone on the block and for three blocks over
and then the names of the people I don't know. I call
them by their house number, by their street address.
I wish they not be sick. I wish they not get shot. I wish.
It calms me but also is it selfish? Do I do it to keep
myself alive? I have a theory that if I let the light
out into the world then we'll all get to stay alive. Want
to stay alive. I think of everything I know about all
the people on my block. I list Ms. Edna and her children.
I say the names of everyone at the church and then
the people I don't know. I want everyone to have money.
I want everyone to have a house and food and be
believed in and be told they're believed in. I want
to know these things can happen so I don't want to die.
Or so I can feel the hollow part of me filling with all
of us getting to be filled up. There's no part of me that's
a saint. I'm not saying this to get some extra credit.
I'm saying I wonder if you do it too? My bones on top
of your bones on top of your bones. Or your bones
on top of mine. All of us awake at 3 a.m. wishing the best
for people like filling up an endless cistern with light
and understanding. All the way down to the center of
the earth and up to where the solitary planes fly past.

Miss you. Would like to shoot some hoops with you.

for Oliver Baez Bendorf

Don't have to be dead for me to miss you.
Miss you. Would like to shoot some hoops
with you. Ask you to teach me
how to shoot buckets with ease. Wish you
could show me your layup. Your alley-oop.
How to tussle without getting hurt. What chain
are you wearing? You know I want one too.
Thick as licorice and gleaming. Wish you
could help me be the flyest guy on the court.
Don't bring any body but your own. You're perfect.
Wish we could wear matching basketball shorts,
high-five all the folks on the benches. Trash-talking
bravado the sun is so in love with us I'm Greek
like a Giannis. My sneakers come from Mount Olympus.
I'm the fiercest porcupine in the den. Pal,
let's drink from bright fountains. Light drips
from our stubbly chins. Miss you. Barreling down
the court. Bouncing. Look at us living. Imagine.

Jessye Norman Cistern Time to Dress for Fall

for Randall Kenan

"The best of friends are sure to part one day."
I can't remember who said it but it's true. I wish
the little church next door were there in person
so I could hear them singing. I really do.
I took my light body out to see and marveled
at the white clapboard and the door. The red
shingle roof's covered with moss since no
one's here to see it. Dust to dust. Or shingle to
moss. The chimney's leaning toward the ground.
We didn't know if they would like us, me
and Angeline. Little church next door in
North Carolina. Pentecostal. I invited the pastor
and his wife to tea. Like my grandmother taught me.
Turns out we like each other very much.
Randall, I was supposed to write another poem.
But let's be honest we know I haven't written
in two years. Or maybe more. I've been trying.
I've been taking the bus and listening to Jessye
Norman. This is where I'm supposed to acknowledge
the pandemic. And how long it's been
since I've ridden the bus. Two friends
have died in the last three weeks and neither
one from COVID. What a stupid sounding
word to cram into a poem. One time my
grandfather told me how Jessye Norman
sang so well that all the cast behind her
was crying in . . . was it Vienna? I was really
young. He used to drive me on the tractor
while we listened to her singing on the outdoor
speakers and I'd think how nice it would be

to be so good at something you'd make
everyone stand still and cry. For joy. For
wonder. I've been trying what seems my
whole life since I stopped writing to describe
the feeling of waking up in the darkness
to the feeling of my grandmother's mink
coat tickling my cheek. Her leaning down
to kiss me after the four-hour drive home
from the opera. You would not tell me, *Think*
about the minks. Though we would of course
know about the minks. Time passes. If I said
She smelled like Oscar de la Renta you'd know
just what I mean. And I could tell you how I
sat behind my grandfather on the tractor
listening to *Les Troyens* and you'd know
just what I mean. I'd say, "What is happening now?"
at the top of my lungs. Not knowing French.
And my grandfather would say, "Everyone's dead
but the ushers." Or. "Things are going from bad
to worse." His voice rising over the engine. Which he'd
cut at just the right moment so we could sit
in the stillness and listen to her. Still alive.
"Cassandra on the wall." He'd say. And I'd say,
"What's that?" And he'd say, "That's when
no one will listen." The smell of late autumn
grass in my nostrils. I'd rest my head on his
back. It must have been a replay or a recording
because she sang that in winter. Or maybe
it's been so long I just don't remember right
at all. I used to sit on the bus and listen
to Jessye Norman before the world got sick.
But the world's always been sick. As long
as I've known it, I mean. I texted, "Do you
know when she sings that song, 'The Summer

Knows'?" And you said, "I do." I'd wait
up as long as I could for her to come up
and kiss me. But I was always surprised.
Little minks. Horrible. But also. I'd do
anything. Literally anything to feel my grandmother
kiss me again. I'd ask, "Was she wonderful?"
And she'd say, "We'll tell you in the morning."
I miss everyone and feel so lonely it's
like an empty opera house inside me.
Like all the chandeliers just shattered
on the floor. I figured I'd just speak plainly.
It's time to dress for fall.

My Perimenopausal Body Cistern Disappointing How Surprising

Bled all day. Stopped bleeding. Bled some more.
Went to the doctor who reached inside the woman
body I try to live with: make peace with: but also ignore.
Sad tenant, my uterus. One day the tenant turned
out to be my landlord. All day I wonder what
it means, clock I know as well as I know anything
but also never wanted. And also won't give up.
In the history of my light body it will show I could
have been another. The shots, the surgeon's
blade. That freedom. But I hold on. Not out of fear.
Well maybe but also: this body I fought for. Timid
skin sack that grew into a kind of magnificence I'd
not expected. I tie my bow tie around my neck that's not
quite the neck I want. But still: the neck survived:
hours on the floor begging for my life: bent
head crying in the bathroom: bent head walking
by the boys yelling, hog and dog and ugly as an animal.
It's confusing. I protect the breasts that I live without
in my mind's eye. I look for hours
at men's trousers and kimonos and bleed all day.
My mind says: Take it out. And though
it's one step closer to one true self I wanted, also
I'd miss it in ways I can't explain. Burnt-off scroll.
I'm a mirror of a mirror. When I was eight at daycare
my friends pulled me aside to talk about a "sex change":
all of us in our Catholic uniforms: Meg, Emily,
Nadine, and Brian who got kicked out because of me.
That's later in the story. We drew me in the sand.
We planned and wondered how much it cost
to be another body. But now? I know my body.
I pull up my pants and feel the lack of one thing
as the muffin top reminds me of the persistence

of another. Me who's with me always.
This pillow that looked over me. Pillow
of skin and fat that I'd call Rubenesque.
It tried its best. To cover me. So I worry over it.
Strange companion. This body that covers me.
And bleeds all day without ceasing. I say, Come on.
I say, Stop. Like I used to when I'd get too scared
of one thing or another. God comes back
to find me in the most confounding ways.
Me and my body. Who are often not the same.

Lent Cisterns: Could I Ever Write a Poem Again After These Years of Bleeding These Years of Mourning?

[Deep Listening is] listening to everything all the time, and reminding yourself when you're not. But going below the surface too, it's an active process. It's not passive. I mean hearing is passive in that soundwaves hinge upon the eardrum. . . . You can do both. You can focus and be receptive to your surroundings. If you're tuned out, then you're not in contact with your surroundings. . . . You have to process what you hear. Hearing and listening are not the same thing.

Pauline Oliveros

I want to keep learning, keep exploring, keep doing more.

Jessye Norman

1

Ash Wednesday

Went into the church for my ashes,
no one was there. Just the organ playing
though I couldn't see who was playing.
I hadn't been in forever. I wondered
if I had to kneel. I didn't remember.

Outside, all the little graves. Wintered
in even though the earth has barely
frozen this year.

2

Let My Story Fall Away Behind Me

Let the past fall away
in order to focus
on the edgeworthia's
redolent bloom. The bees
map the air outside
the bee box. Satchels
of pollen heavy on
their furry legs.
It's hard, isn't it, not
to look backward?
To let the story
live outside myself.
Have I ever
made a poem
that didn't look
inward? Do I know
a story worth
telling about the earth?

3

Light Steeples Ice

The garden snowed over snowed in covering
the graves all the chimneys collaborating all the
ruckus of those pilgrims' bones under the city
built street by brittle street the cow path the field
the __________ to talk about the __________
overhear the meadowlark on one's way lost in
the marsh grass   not making it to church
brick by brick curb by curb place of worship the
workhouse I stared out the window dazzled by
the ice on the trees dazzled which means (*of
a bright light*) *blind* (*a person*) *temporarily:* I
saw my bones rising up through the snow saw
version after version of my body make its way to
church all the while wishing for the field that's
my legacy dutiful and furious about it offering
my back to the wheel.

4

Winter Nocturne

Solo in the empty
house everyone's gone
the cat couldn't scoot
out fast enough house
like a kettle house
light a gong and me
inside its belly
oh to lie in bed with you
up here we'd lusten
as the snow falls
as windows
thicken with
crystals little cat
mousing by glisten
of moonlight
streetlight icelight
beneath

5

After the Party

All those years my not
talking about it. But all of us knowing.

You know, the things he'd say.

The record clicking till
someone walked across the room to
stop it.

Ice in the highball clinking as
he walked across the room to stop it.

I'd touch the place the bullet
went through. I'd think of him lying
in the square left for dead.

I know how to someone if I
have to.

How do I know how to do
that?

I know how to say
so someone feels so scared
they can't even get up from the floor.

6

"Write the Best Thing That's Happened Today"

I'm finding new paths
to the sweetness. I'm avoiding
negative self-talk. I'm writing
one poem a day.

7/8

From Saint Mary's

for Lucille Clifton

1

highway in darkness,
strip malls, wheat
bright in the fields,
i thought it was snow
but the driver said, *it's been*
eighty degrees here. Amish
families somewhere past
the dark car. are the horses
asleep? outline of
buggies in moonlight.
soft lamps in the milking
barn as warm as a yolk in
its shell. i looked skyward
for jupiter conjunct venus:
the driver endlessly talking,
a river of christian rock on
the radio: there is always
always another chance.

2

i can feel the lump
and i don't want to feel it
not after all the months
the almost full year of blood
everywhere all the time.
i want to think about

the kayaks and sailboats
i sat by today as i ate
a simple salad and drank
unsweetened iced tea.
lord just let the little things
rule me for a while.
why does the body
always come knocking
when i've had the perfect
day. why does it turn
every party into a rehearsal
for my funeral. every
celebration into a eulogy.
i should remember
the best part of the day:
pouring dressing on the lettuce,
ice in the glass that kept being
refilled, lucille clifton's
daughters' hands holding mine
as we listened to a recording
of blessing the boats.

whatever is waiting for me
will have to wait a while longer.

9

(of the eyes) be affected by a bright light:

Late in the day I feel them straining. Little instruments pushed past their breathing point. Or. Pushed past their warp and weft. Past the place of vision and into pragmatic weariness. Weariness deep behind the eye. The cistern in the back of the head up into the orbital bones into the _______ I don't even know what resides there. I guess the brain. Too hard to edit anymore and write poems (I misspell *anymore* six times fumbling enough so even autocorrect can't make sense of it anymore). Some days I wish I knew something else I could do with my body that would pay the bills. Sun's going down now. I should have left the spellimg erroes and just let my body have a break.

10

“Did you hear the news out of Tennessee out of North Carolina out of”

I know you
know they I
know you
know but also I don’t
think you do I want
to explain it more
clearly because you
say I live in a
cistern of peace.

There is no peace in
my heart

no march no
brunch and no party
up in the club of my
four chambers

the amp is nothing
but feedback

so I can barely write
or dream or lose this
weight I’m meant to
lose my blood
pressure’s out of
control.

Did you hear what’s
up in

they stripped away the
birdsong they took
the owl out of the oak
tree they took the oak
tree too

took my canopy
and all the brightness
I can muster.
Wayne Shorter up
and died. I mean
everybody's sick of
this earth.

11

(of the eyes) be affected by a bright light:

9:28 p.m.: too far gone even for autocorrect

Nystagmus Variation

Oh little light body it's fine. Look at all the saxophones waiting for you on the pathway :: gleaming and making their flower songs. It won't matter what you can see or what ouu can't see. Your eyes won't huret all the time anymore. I know it's gets late and they get so tireds. It gets hard to see the flower of yourself anymore. Let the horns bring you home. Remember when the ground the trees the waters that rushed past gleamed with the music you made. No one loved you then or if they did you didn't know it. But look at you then. Survicinh. Its that hour of the day where it's hard to make sense of anything. Where half of what you write I spelled wronf. It's olay. Even Dexter Gordon had his hard days I bet. Days

when the notes jumbled up to nothing. Kep
going. Just keep going into the cistern of
yourself and the muic will come. You can ,ake
anything fill with light when you sign long
enough. It doesn't have to be lour. Put your
mouth to the mouthpiece of the world and
ungold.

12

The Well the Reel

Every room's a castle
bedroom if you make it luxe
enough. Piles of pillows, throws,
maybe a fake fur that reminds
you of a bear or some other
animal who could keep you warm.
What's an animal you'd like
to curl up with? Little
garret 700 miles
from home: I've got my
little bed with its headboard
and its footboard made of
oak. I've got the pillows
and the quilts and the comforters.
I've got the linens and
even got the cat who's curled
up on the nubbly caftan Jen
and Oliver and Jenny got me
before surgery. I've got the
Himalayan salt lamp and Nikky's
hooked rug of the owl. Little
Christmas lights all over my
desk. I found them at CVS
when I was feeling lonely
and filled to the gullet
with darkness. I'm
writing this now under
the covers on the twelfth
day of Lent. Just riffing
just reeling as Pauline

Oliveros plays. A cistern
can fill up with anything
you can think of. Sweetest
custard or ash. Today
I walked to the bus
to go hear Irish
music and ended up at
the taiyaki shop instead. Watching
a pancake get molded
to the shape of a fish
then filled with custard
as I drank my sencha.
Marvelous. Marveling.

13

Hawk Song Cistern

I think about him on the cross. I did when I was little too. But then not until this moment when hawk song outside my winter window. Heard it in passing. Loud right in the middle of the pane then fading off past the steeple of the First Church. I'm not sure why it made me think of him. Who I believe was him, though no more the ______ of God than all of us. Too much pain probably to have heard a hawk song. Too much fear and calling out. Somehow when the bird flew past I wondered was it sunny like today is. So bright and me with a little cold. Which has my mind wandering. It smells like winter but outside? Spring's blanket drapes all over me. How far could I reach my arms out? How much could I bear? And would I hear the hawk that flew past me? That poor young man.

14

"Write the Best Thing That's Happened Today"

Oh the moon! Full moon in Virgo and
soon after, Saturn entered Pisces. It's
not like I could see that transit happen
but I sure saw the moon. Saw it between
the branches as I walked to the Red Line
from the $7 showing of *The Quiet Girl*
and, after, a great bowl of matzo ball soup.
Luxury. That's the word all the olders
were using at the theater as they marveled
over the seats that reclined.

Luxury!
one woman said after her friend yelled,
I need a demonstration! to her
who came over to help her out.
I was reading my book in my own seat.
Sipping my tea and waiting for
Elizabeth. I ate some candy, which I'd
given up for Lent. I didn't enjoy it that much.
I am getting the Lenten in a way I haven't
before. I'm learning. Which is what
Saturn in Pisces is supposedly about.
Two and a half years to commit to loving
and working hard at the things that you
want. But also: Learn your lesson.
The moon was so big between the buildings.
It was cold but I didn't mind so much.

15

Wild Strawberries Far as the Eye Can See

after *Steven Universe* and my students

I, too,
have a
red gem
in my
middle,
yes, a
wild
strawber
ry far as
the eye
can
see it
goes
into me
deeper
than my
bones
or my
organs
or my
skin
sack.
My red
gem
portals
into the
wheelba
rrow of

my
deepest
wants
and
memori
es:
sitting
on the
roof
of the
garage,
plucking
berries
first
thing in
the
morning
.
Writing
my first
poem in
the
Scooby-
Doo
noteboo
k
I got at
Ben
Franklin
. My red
gem.
My wild
strawber
ry goes

to the
before
I had a
body in
anybody
else's
mind
but
mine. It
goes
past the
worn
seat of
the
confessi
onal to
spring
morning
s on the
basketb
all
court,
those
sweet
days
without
school
or
anyone.
My
gem.
My wild
strawber
ry the

sweetne
ss so
particula
r:
nubbly
and
barely
able to
be held
between
two
fingers
but oh
the
sweetne
ss lasts
all day.

16

After Fred Wah's Pickerels After Puncturing My Eardrum on the Plane

blew my ear out on the plane
too tentative to spray the medicine up my nostril
now under blankets half a world of birdsong

ear and I suppose the other's also full of
I can't hear which doesn't mean it isn't
there   at the bee box they're bearding
too early in the year

it's not really that warm out
what do I know
planted borage nettle
mountain mint
turns out they love poison ivy

17

Jessye Norman Shun Lee Palace Variation

Jessye Norman

left the Met,

after she finished

her work for the evening

in the first act

of *Les Troyens.*

She left

to go eat Chinese food

at Shun Lee Palace

with her family,

and then came back

for the rest of the opera

and to receive

her applause.

If there is anything

that's happened today

that's been more pleasurable

than learning that fact

I cannot remember

what on Earth it was.

Maybe breathing oxygen was better.

Maybe standing upright.

Not really.

Imagine.

18

(of a bright light) blind (a person) temporarily:

Discard the ice let the spring
bubble up! Let cherry blossoms
balloon and fall and fall along
the koi pond! Hold my hand
as we walk in the city park
wishing for another kind of life,
not that we don't love ours: here:
but what if we could find ourselves
a little different topography
to grow in? I'm tired
of living near the mills
that poisoned us the railroad
tracks that ferry chemicals
from one town to the next.
Even if I still find the train's
horn romantic in the dark
of night, I think I'd rather
live and just remember
how we used to love it
so close by. We couldn't
even get the camera to
recognize the cherry blossoms,
they were so bright against
the sun. There's just us
smiling, me with a cold
that almost kept us in but
I thought come on let's
go out into it. Us and
half the city reflected
in the blossom light.

We like this life alright
but also the blossoms:
can they help us see
toward something
different?

19

Wildflowers on the ground, bears and wolves in the hills

Nettles and bee balm. Borage mellowing
into chamomile in my eye's cistern.
And the sun pouring over it pouring
over the field. I'd like to live someplace
nicer than where we do now. Greener,
also less gunfire. Less sorrow everywhere.
I grew up with sorrow everywhere.
And the screaming, the yelling, the threats
that I was supposed to take as a joke.
Where did he learn it? Where does
anyone learn to say pass me the   or
I'll   your   ? Bees everywhere,
I imagine. On the yarrow, the nettle,
pink hawk's-beard. *Crepis rubra.*
Song rising from the grasses
from the blooms as I walk without
a sidewalk or a path.

20

"What brought me the most pleasure today?"

After days of congestion I could finally smell the onions Angeline was cooking. I was sitting in the front room with the cat on my lap. Skewed leftward toward the poem. The house had gotten so cold! The cat's fur was freezing. We'd just turned the clocks toward spring. The cat getting warmer as I wrote.

I'm trying to do these little variations. These small poems that maybe could bloom out to something. Each one on a different day of Lent. A different part of the journey. Someone said, But that's not giving something up. I don't know. I think the act of just making something each day is giving up self-hatred. Giving up the loathing that says I can't make anything anymore. It's almost spring, isn't it? Cherry blossoms drifting on the koi pond. The cat's fur warming. This cup of tea waiting as I work.

21

Ring

To get outside
of my head and its
incessant ringing.
Not philosophical:
got on the plane
with a cold. And now?
A head full of cherry
blossoms. Ringing.

Rings in the trunk of the oak
we cut down in the
fall. Endless circles.
Now the owls don't
come to make a nest
inside the hollow. My ear
:: muffled. The desire
for quality has silenced
me anyway.

Could I just love it
again? My fingers moving
along the keyboard. The
shape a poem can make
on the page.

22

Occoneechee Speedway Hearing the Layers

for Daniel

Not sure how this one will go yet. I walked
to the iron gate from the car park across
town. We'd miscommunicated. So I
was on my own for part of the stroll. I tried
to listen for all of the layers. Could I hear
birdsong? How many birdsongs? Could I
tell how big the bird was and in what direction?

I try not to get anxious. I remember the layers.
Lying in my bed all those years ago
after my mind broke. My mind still breaks
in the darkness. A book said to listen
and decipher every single thing you could hear.
And it did calm me. To hear birds waking up.
The traffic starting to build. I could hear my
breathing and the cat's breathing and if I went
deep enough inside, the gut
machinery of the building: pipes, electricity,
someone flushing a toilet somewhere.
Each layer actually there and not
the voices I was waiting to tell me
          what? I don't know. And when
they asked what I was afraid of hearing.
Was it voices? Whose? Once
I was walking down Ashby and heard
a branch break. I hit the ground
and stayed there beneath a rosemary
bush for what felt like an hour.

This morning I woke to that feeling
again. *What if?* My muddled ear
working its way to some articulation.
I listened and breathed. I prayed.
And again today, with you, old friend.
I listen. I try to hear the layers.

23

Muffled Chime

If it's not one thing it's another. If it's not the bleeding it's the bother of my ear not working. Now I hear only half the wind chime. But also I only half hear when I argue with my neighbor. Not so much argue as *discuss.* I half discuss and feel my heart pound harder. Want my half. Of the driveway. How ridiculous. I want it fully. Can't hear much of what he's saying but I feel all of my hunger. Life is half wind chime and then all that wanting. When did I learn to want so much? A driveway. A house. A car. A   .
A   . One after another I add them up. Cistern that never reaches the lip of itself. Just gets deeper and deeper. Today I watched the cat wake up and run all the way to the back porch because a squirrel was on the stump. I didn't even hear it. But I get the hunger. Little squirrel

looking for all the acorns it hid way back in autumn. Half of the birdsong. Half of the hawk flying overhead.

24

Eleanor of Aquitaine

I don't even know how to make language
for the swarm today! Glimmering chalice
cupping the magnolia leaf. Jackson came
to get them. Found the Virgin Queen and
held her out to us. Then placed her in a
box and one by one all the swarm
dropped toward her. The second swarm
in weeks, which means the Elder Queen
absconded with her retinue. *Does that
mean she's wild now?* I asked. *Because
we didn't see so you couldn't come and
catch her.* Yes, he said. It did.

Imagine her. Like Eleanor of Aquitaine.
No more than a mile away. Luxurious
hollow or attic. A forgotten
bee box. Resplendent next door
in the abandoned house. How great
to just move in when you see an open
vessel. Not have to pay or ask permission.

To fill the empty vessel with life as the
vessel should be filled.

I could watch them forever. Not needing
me at all.

25

Mill Cistern Wheel Returning

Cog? Wheel? What was the source
of it. We watched them turning
but I heard them first, amid
the muffled world.

I can always hear
the river. Even when I can't hear
what you're saying right next to me

I can hear the rapids.
Can tell a gully in the water
from the stronger current.

Was that traffic in the distance, I
asked. Just some frequency.
Someone's motor. We walked
on for a little longer. We stopped
and turned around.

26

Just the Facts Practice: Sunday Night

I'm nervous to give the talk about
Mary Oliver.

It was just supposed
to be a lunch but now it's in an
auditorium and there's live-streaming.

I don't even know how to talk
about queerness anymore.

So how did I get in this mess of talking
about it in relation to Mary Oliver?

What if for thirty-five minutes I talk
about the waterfall?

And sitting on the rocks by the river beside
my mother's first house?

Reading her green *Selected* next
to the house where my mother
lived before she met my father.

Before she had me.

There's a picture of her the day
she bought the house with her
first husband.

She's peering in the window,

a black cat is walking past.

I don't want to talk about my mother
in poems anymore.

It's like that poem "Dogfish" says

except I'm the one
who doesn't want to hear about it.

Is that the truth?

Next door the new neighbors are spending their
second night here.

I think we'll plant a wall of rosemary between us.

The soft animal something something

loves what it loves.

27

Wind in the Ear

Out into the bright light from the train. All around me cars and into the bright light dazzled :: in my eardrum. The cistern of the ear or is it the cistern of the world. Into my light body. I walked by the graveyard with a warm taiyaki in my hand.

And the wind pouring through my ear canal or should I say it was a breeze. It didn't hurry. No. It didn't hurry or hurt as it entered but I could feel all I wasn't hearing. This was temporary. My ear cistern full of fluid.

Also the day itself. And making art out of it. Fleeting. Light on the gravestones. Fleeting. And my own light body three months out from surgery. Seemingly better but who knows what's growing. The graveyard backs up to the windows of the pizza place.

I kept leaning in and saying, I'm sorry I can't hear you. Dazzled by the sweetness of the white-bean paste touching the   (what is the way to talk about the pleasure and specificity of the dough) of the taiyaki.

Little fish. I watched them pour the batter and place two perfect balls of white-bean paste. Six minutes then they flipped it. What? I said as the woman laughed and handed it to me. I was so grateful. That perfect paper envelope it came in. Warm in my hand.

28

An Inn for the Coven

Witch hazel going wild along the
walkway. And all the spots to sit and
read our spell books. And all the
ways to keep the   out. Two black
cats and a beaver who eats carrots all
day. Every room an upper room
even on the ground floor. And bee
boxes in the way way back. And the
sweet man who comes to keep them.
All our loves are witches too. Or
warlocks. All our children and all
our children. Welcome. Water
running in the brook. Clean enough
to drink from our hands. And seven
sources. And a deep well. All for us
and all for those we bring over. Four
swings in the branches. A library in
every hollow. And birds. So many
birds we stop trying to name them.
Will just let them be with their own
names. Maybe they'll tell us.
Porches. Tomatoes in the summer
and pumpkins in the fall. And curry
leaves and curry blossoms. Jasmine
in the rooms at night. All loves
protected. All of us playing cribbage
on the lawn.

29

River Light Walk Across the River

Light body crossing
the bridge light body
over the water. All
the boats out and one
overturned. Sail on
the water but nobody
seeming to panic.

Watched the body
simply right itself and
another one pulled
on the rope.
Watched another
one come up from
the water. No sirens.

No screaming. Just
light and the wind
ruffling the river.
Like a slip thrown on
the bed my
grandmother used to
say about the river

below. Current a
fabric current a
shimmer. I watched
the body right itself
and another wait for
it to come up from

the water. I saw the
brass knocker on the
tower. I saw the body
righting itself.

30

Harbor O Pioneers

bowl of mountain	bowl of skull	endless pelvic gong

and everywhere the sun	lapping over the bowl	or dipping beneath it

I want a full opening	every part of me	gold pooling

absurd in its bounty	and the green	astonishing

everyone looking up	from their picnic	from the baseball game

it's been so long	since I've been	equinox

31

One Bright Room

One bright room to grow your love in. One bright room to let the sun flood in. To fill you up. A room to make spaghetti carbonara for all your friends assembled. A plate for the old dog, a piece of bacon for the cat. Maybe the younger dog is pregnant. She'll need a whole bowl for herself. A room where it's not wasteful because everyone has enough and a little bit more. Fill a bowl for all your animals. For your own animal self most of all. Let the love flood in. Kids playing soccer or football or cricket outside the window. The windows are huge! You see for blocks and count all the steeples and mosques. Everyone fasting for Ramadan and at night the sound of feasting. All the strangers coming through the open city's doors. Jasmine everywhere. A thousand boats bobbing on the shore.

32

No Poems Today

Because you're here. There's warm
bread to be eaten. With cheese and jam.
Small shops to walk into and look around
just for the pleasure of looking with
you. We spend hours with the seed
catalogue imagining a place bigger
than ours. I buy more seeds than
we'll ever be able to use but here's
hoping. Opening a package of seeds
in three weeks (they come all the way
from Canada!) you'll say, "This
is too many seeds!" But come on.
Let's be here for the bounty. I can
still imagine years of possibility
ahead of us. A place with just a little
more space for us to stretch out.
A new economy and, yes, I know
I can't drive at night. But who needs
to go anywhere in the future. Maybe
friends will come over. Imagine how
nice to hear nothing but the stars.

33

All My Friends, Assemble!

In the amphitheater of my sternum
let your whiskers sweep a symphony.
In my pelvic floor plant hyacinth
and pea blossom. Bring tea. The most
vegetal you can find. Steep it in the welcome
cistern of my skull. How long have I been
gone now? What stories of everything
you've done in the in-between. Lay
an egg or fifty. Hide an acorn where
the marrow used to glisten. Does marrow
glisten? I know I glisten now. Golden
fungus all around you. I'm here. Let
the bear lumber and dig into me. Take
me to the next story someone will tell.

34

Miss you

You told me the
trees are budding
but since you got
on the plane I can't
see it. I'm full of
sadness and bile.
Put my earphones
on and dance
around the room.
But my bones
won't do it. What's
spring without you?
A hollow dumpling.
Asparagus
oversteamed: pale
and just disgusting.
Who cares about
the river with its
shimmers and
pleasant current?
Not me.
Misanthrope at the
coffee shop. Forget
about how vegetal
the green tea is.
Told the barista I
didn't really feel the
grasslands today. I
tried to taste the

spring moss in the
cup. No luck.

35

Moss Ear Writing Date with Ezra

for Ezra Zwaeli

It's green imagination I'm going for. Ruffled
mound along the rock face transformed into

something. My fingers grasped
the emerald carpet so I wouldn't fall into the Eno.

I want the cistern and the earth that surrounds.
The symphony coming up from inside,

the ground speaks to me if I can let myself
hear. Moss ear listening. The subtle tube shivers

with pleasure even when it feels to me like nothing's
come through. *Listen* is different from *Hear.*

I can still do the first, I tell myself, even if
the pressure on the plane sucked my eardrum

till it popped through the membrane.
I can't *hear* so well. But, moss ear to the ground,

to the cistern I can listen. Ezra sits across
the table from me mouthing his sestina—

it doesn't matter whether I hear it. Though I want
to hear and feel my left ear reach out

to the nothing, to the muffle. The part
that's compromised is the part that wants

to know. My right ear could care less:
lets its cistern pool with bossa nova,

the barista dropping ice into a glass. Bags
open to a parliament of hands. *I'm a lawyer*

one man says to another who says *Mm.*
The right ear listens the sunlight in while

the left ear strains and reaches, bullied
by desire for its own articulation. Meanwhile

birds sing somewhere. Moss creeps:
Sunday solo of a slide trombone. The frogs
can hear it from the water. Water bugs

let their pencil legs caress it. That's what
I want knowledge to be. Ezra is working out

the pattern, his hand covering his head as the bass
plays on the speakers. I can tell he doesn't

want to do it anymore. Not right now. But also
moss ear listens to him keeping on. On a break

from his day job, forehead on the table. Listen,
it's fucking hard to have a job. I'm trying

to coax the earth below the floor to meet him,
the mushrooms, tender roots somewhere

below the concrete and the trains. Form a cradle
or a trampoline. Let the body listen for the cistern

and the cistern will open up to meet us. Hands over
the eyes can be frustration. Hands over the eyes can be

a portal to the cathedral of cockroaches. Who don't
know the clock needs to be punched. Or that the world

reviles them. Shimmer of the slick and perfect
carapace the color of this wooden table Ezra puts

his head on. We place our hands along our faces
at the same time. The moss ear perks up. Listens

for the bridge of air and dust, oil and pheromone
our hands release as they cradle our fatigue.

36

"What. Already?"

Already it's been a good day.
Lent. How many times have I thought

of Christ on the cross? More than
usual I think I'd say. The pain

of it, sure. How the sky might have looked.
Also, oddly, wondering what was

growing there. Just dust and hardscrabble
earth? Or were there plants of such fragrance:

thyme, oregano, yarrow, which
doesn't smell but in the warmth of spring

blooming has a scent to it. I'm not
thinking of it like a poem or for

a poem. It's not that kind of economy.
I've just been wondering if it smelled

like the hills in Los Angeles I'd
work my way up in the line of

midday hikers. Most of us winded
as we crested the top. Nothing

but sky. Sweat soaking our shirts. The smell?
Mostly dog shit. But then: thyme or brush

or petrichor. Thirty-three seems so
young now. To leave your body. I

wasn't ready. Vessel of light. One
day you're weeding or cupping water

cold from the well. I can't imagine:
was I ever that young?

37

Three Months out from Fibroid Surgery the Best Thing That Happened Today

:: the smell of the ornamental curry plant :: up from the concrete that was warming :: I could feel it warming :: felt grateful :: not the weaponized gratitude of the Wantstagram feed :: not with the blight of shame on it for feeling ::

:: when you "should" be feeling so happy to be alive :: I felt grateful for the smell easing up from the curry :: a smell I can't name but can say :: it rested in the back of my nasal passages :: and the top of my throat :: and also in my eyeballs :: in what I'd call the roof of my eyeballs :: my neighbors' dog Bernard walked up :: he lifted his leg :: Andrea told him to stop but I said :: *why not* :: it's a kind of celebration isn't it :: to mark things :: three months out from surgery :: today the doctor looking at the ultrasound saying :: *I think it's going to be fine.*

38

Path

Little light body always dreaming
of some new path or other. Paving
the path with gold or clover. Come
over and see what it is to want

to be alive. I'm getting used to it
and still sometimes look for ways
to be unhappy. After the doctor
said it was going to be okay I went

and blew out my eardrum. Then
my intestines got squirrelly. My
head hurt. Eighteen months of not
knowing. Ten months of bleeding

most every day from my uterus
out my vagina (a word it's hard
for me to even say in relation
to me) and then I got better.

And then the ear the guts my
head pounding. *The pain needs
somewhere to go,* I reasoned.
But for real? Why should it

keep living inside me? What
about my radiance that God
told me about. Those nights
I'd wake up in the far room

of the house. Wondering why
the bed was spinning. Me

in my footed pajamas with my
camel and my bear. Too scared

to scream. But alone. What
was happening? And then a voice
from the river telling me
I'd be okay. A voice in the

darkness making a light
of me. Pouring my light
into me.

39

Forgiveness I Am Trying

The boys kicked the door.
They kicked the door again
so hard the house shook.
The boys called me *Sir*
but not in a way that made
me feel debonair. The boys
asked if we had daughters
because they wanted to come
in the house and get some
pussy. The boys told me
to go fuck myself. The boys
brought the larger boys
to stand outside our house.

I am trying to remember
it's a time of forgiveness.
I am trying to remember
my body has never been
my home. I wave and water
the garden. I offer the flowers
from the bed. The mint, rosemary,
sure take a few tomatoes,
take whatever you can hold.

Ms. Sylvia lived here for
years and taught the whole
block to garden. People
would bring lawn chairs
out to watch her tend it.
Raymond told me she taught
him everything he knew.

Said she grew snake plants
eight feet tall and brought
them in for winter. His
landlord kicked him out
of the boardinghouse
and then he died of COVID.

I heard from another neighbor
who didn't remember Ms. Sylvia
at all. I can't tell how long it was
before someone lived here before
we did. It was a while. Ms. Edna
said the house was empty and she'd
been tired of babysitting. But still.
It was someone's. It wasn't ours.
Who planted the irises in the back?
Is the pokeweed here because
the birds carried it or because it is
good medicine and salad so someone
had a crop?

From the middle of the earth to the
firmament, I pray in the middle of the
night, to try getting everyone and all
the animals and other breathing things.
I include the water and the rocks.
The owls who'd been here for as long
as Ms. Edna remembers and then
we had to take the willow oak
down. And now they're gone.
When the boys call me Sir
in a way that does not recognize

my attention to my hair and to
my bow tie, I try to remember

it's Lent. When they kick
the door I try to remember
every breath that's been here
before me. C drove past
then pulled her minivan back
to meet me and say how she
grew up in our house and next
door. Her uncle died of AIDS
there. Her aunt held him
in her arms in the driveway.
They'd been living as next-door
neighbors for years.

A new plant pops up that we never
planted and we think, probably
something Ms. Sylvia planted
that got shaded out by the oak.
And now the light comes in
and now the bloom comes forward.
What would Jesus do is a question
I genuinely ask myself. Not a bumper
sticker. A bodhisattva and young
man prone to anger as much as
he was prone to love. What would
that young man do? As the boys

kick the door that was not always
mine. As the boys break the planters.
As the boys call me Sir in a way
that makes my blood run cold. From
the middle of my world to my
firmament. I am trying. I'm not there.

40

Estate

of the belly muscles bending back in the deep stretch after dinner on the couch. Simple pleasure of the back arching and the pull of the abdomen the uterus in its cup of pelvis and the open pelvis. Opening the chest and breathing in deeply. Flexing the shoulders back the sails of my body like a Viking boat. Curve after curve of the body reaching the edge of its instrument as it bends with pleasure. Feel the belly muscles pulling to their pleasures' limit. Which is pleasure entire. Itching with pleasure like a cat. Feel the crackle of the back muscles engaging. The real deep truth of my flanks. Like the butcher strokes in the shop hanging from the hook. Let the pelvis into the stretch. Think of even the uterus opening into the fullness of the breath. It's scary to write it don't worry. You aren't bleeding all over everything all the time anymore. Open up.

Good Friday

All your friends assemble. The cats
curled on laps as you sit at the table.
All the dogs get all the prime rib
they want. No scraps for anyone
because there are no scraps just
heaping portions and everyone
has their fill. All the clocks stop.
The lights strung over the feast
are actually stars. Everyone's
made it through our Saturn returns
like champions. Pour
the nectar into the goblets,
lift your hand for the toast.
Put your shoulder into it. In
the distance you see trees
and past that you see the hilltop.
No one else is looking. They're
wiping saganaki off one another's
chin. They're kissing baklava
from a stranger's lips. Honey
never tasted so good. A little buckwheat
in it. A little borage. The poison
ivy the bee found on its way
home. In your ears the buzzing
as you look into the distance.
Head like a hive. Look away.
Feel your friends' hands on
your shoulders. Sleepy drunk
they're leaning on you, saying
something about some other
night you all had together. Someone
took a goat and cooked it

in the ground. From somewhere
a guitar. Girls laughing or boys
laughing. Why did you ever care
who was who? The point is
they're laughing. In the distance
the hilltop almost looks lit
from behind. But it's not
close to morning? It couldn't
be. All your friends
assembled at the table you
built with your dad. How
he held his hand over yours
as you tapped the hammer.
He smelled like cedar. His
beard tickling your cheek.
Why feel so alone when someone's
just offered you figs, some cheese,
has placed their hand on
the back of your neck. Has turned
your chin away from the view
in the distance. *Be here, right
now,* they say. Leaning in
to kiss your mouth.

Holy Saturday

(of the eyes) be affected by a bright light:

Yes. Through the trees. Everyone finished feasting. The wine almost gone. Just the blush in the glasses. Somewhere guitars playing together. Light singing. What was the song? You almost remember. That sweet boy's voice. Or was it a girl? Why did it matter? It didn't matter. A sweet voice singing then joined by another. Hey lolly lolly. Over and again. Sometimes someone laughing. Stopping the song. Then starting again. A hand on your shoulder. That sweet weight. Someone lifts themselves up. To go to the tree line. To the edge of the courtyard. To the shadowed corner. Where someone is waiting. Through the trees the hill blazing. Can you see it you asked. Your friend asleep on the table lifted their head. No. Only the stars. Jasmine everywhere. All of a sudden. The first night of bloom. Your friend dancing in the light of the fire. Your friend asleep with their head on the table. Your friend staring toward the hillside. Looking at you. Then looking away.

41

Every Day but Sunday

Four more days of
Lent and I wrote
through the Sundays
I was meant to take
off. But what a gift to
spend 41 days of
observation. Who
am I today? Well,
my eyes hurt. The
plane was on time
but I felt late as I sat
on the T waiting to
get to the office.

Two kids talked
about "Europe
skiing" and their
housekeepers. I
thought about Lent.
Thought about
Christ on the cross.
That's not true. I
wanted to bash my
head against the
shatterproof glass of
the window and
walk out through the
tunnels.

But later I did think
about him. As I
walked up from the
train and past the
graves awash in
sunlight, right there
in the middle of the
city late afternoon.
How tired he must
have been by the
time they hoisted
him up.

Just exhausted. Not
the son of God any
more than the rest
of us, though maybe
he thought so. I
don't know. 33
seems a lifetime ago
at this point. I was
still a kind of child. I
believed good would
out in the end
without me even
trying.

I keep thinking of
wiping sweat from
his brow or telling
him
I don't even
know what. When I
was 33 I spent a lot

of time with my
head in my hands.
Walking around Los
Angeles feeling
blessed by the sun

and jacarandas and
endless swimming
pools. Also lonely
beyond measure.
And also like I was
meant to
                    I
don't even know
what.

42

Every Day but Sunday

The best thing about the day
was talking about baseball.
Thinking about baseball.

Getting the tickets and
deciding poems matter
but also so does baseball.

Meetings tomorrow
can just take a powder. All
day I imagined the green

of the outfield, the hat I'll get
since it will be 43 degrees
at 2 p.m. in Boston. Already

it's tomorrow in my mind.
Taking the Green Line.
Getting a hot cup of

something for my hands. God
I love a day game. It feels
like what I thought life would be

growing up. Just freedom
and nobody yelling at you
to get moving. I hope it

smells like peanuts and popcorn
and sauerkraut. I don't even
care who wins. Or maybe I do.

But God, I just think well I just think
thank you for this poem and all the days
of baseball. I didn't think I'd make it.

Not here like this. I thought
I'd never be happy again.

43

Every Day but Sunday

Formless as a cloud building or
Dispersed as on April's pollen, eyes
Blooming Open open shaking
side to side As is their want. My
head Lolls back and forth on the stem
From my shoulders Justin comes through
the side gate fields of him if I
take my glasses off he's everywhere
look we're trumpet and corona
one body and box full of bees
where he's headed the smoke from the
smoker that covers us both wax
some pine needles whatever he
has around it makes us smell like
church I say lulled leave my glasses
off I'm all petals and nectar
we're one hum one gold breeze into
the colony that eases heals
kills reforms itself around us
I inhale lean into golden
musk of us assembled what if
this was all my body my stem
my bulb my roots my endlessness.

44

Every Day but Sunday

Today I felt sick of it I felt tired
today the marzipan banana didn't help
and the herbs in the Nepali food that
I couldn't name only did so much
a little but not enough I felt sick
of people even most people I love
and I didn't want to keep making
small talk I just didn't want to I was
tired of the endless etiquette of New
England even the marzipan apple
the woman slipped in the box and
the obscene amount of jam on the strawberry
Danish didn't help every poem I thought
of starting already had an ending so
they were dead in the water before I'd
even started the light through the bare
branches just pissed me off the sweet
bookseller who was nothing but
wonderful I could barely button my
pants and thought what if I just let
it all go as I ate the Danish I mean
I was really angry and feeling sorry
for myself the sun poured in the windows
I hadn't bled in three months
and was so full of rage with the light
shining all over me I mean I literally
was suffused with light I had to squint
as I wrote this there was nothing
but bounty and yes the terror of it
starting again the endless bleeding

the pads the diapers the never
sleeping even two hours straight
in the night but this day was nothing
but marzipan iced green tea a light-
filled office with nothing to do
but write poems and still I hated
my life and everyone with such
a blazing fury I couldn't help
this lack of gratitude as I bit
into the marzipan that the woman
and I had spoken at such length
about the sun all over me
this absolute empire of being alive

45

Every Day but Sunday

First night at the Met. Everyone's
been waiting for her to come sing.
A Monday. *Les Troyens*
is fucking *five hours long.*

I wonder what she ordered.
Before heading back to her standing ovation.

I remember lobster dumplings.
Swimming by in their glistening carts.
My grandmother smelled of Chanel.
She placed my napkin on my lap.

It wasn't that night that we went there.
But still.
Luxury.
It hurts to recall.

All of it lost.
Jessye Norman.
My grandparents.
Our rickety chariot.

Making its way home through the night.

46

Every Day but Sunday

I like how the crowd swayed
and the layered greens how they
welcomed me. Reminded of the best
parts of childhood like how the
stadium smelled: peanuts roasted
with honey all over, beer,
hot dogs, a bathroom somewhere
in the distance. It sounds gross but
it was a sweetness. People
brought blankets including
Jill and Tim who called
my name as I was looking around
for them. I wish I could afford
every day game there is. But today
was a jewel even if it's the last
time. All the kids on the jumbotron,
seeing themselves and jumping
like crazy. The feel of the cold
air: 43 but felt like 36, all of us
shivering together. Giddy with
it. Rain that was a little thicker,
almost snow, against my face
as we walked back along
the river. Listening to the
crews row past, cutting the
water, and the *shush shush*
shush of the oars but thicker
almost like a thresher through
wheat. And over the bridge
down the street. Into the pizza

place, tang of garlic and tomato
in the back of my throat
just from the smell of it.
I missed you. I wish you
were here.

Notes

"Reawakening Cistern: Recovering the Golden Thread" appeared in *Energy in All Directions,* Tang Museum, Skidmore College.

"Miss you. Would like to grab that chilled tofu that we love." is for Jenny Tone-Pah-Hote. Her book *Crafting an Indigenous Nation: Kiowa Expressive Culture in the Progressive Era* (University of North Carolina Press) is just one part of her extraordinary legacy.

"An Inn for the Coven" appeared in *You Are Here: Poetry in the Natural World,* edited by Ada Limón.

Acknowledgments

This book, these poems, took almost a decade to write. They could not have been written without the friends, neighbors, readers, animal familiars, strangers, and every other being that kept me going. Without the land.

For those dear neighbors and friends who sustained me through illness, who sent food, notes, poems, watched BritBox, made me cake, sent me kaftans, who kept asking me about my work in ways that felt truly supportive, who took walks with Angeline after my surgery, who cared for us when I lived up in Cambridge, who got me through COVID in the midst of recovering from longer-term illness. Who reminded me I was a poet when I needed the reminder. Thank you beyond words: Oliver Baez Bendorf, Jenny Johnson, Jennifer Chang, Evan Rhodes, Desi Rhodes-Chang, Hank Rhodes-Chang, Ross Gay, Adrian Matejka, Kim Henry, Ms. Edna Bell and the Bell family, Michelle Robinson, Ian Morse, Heidi Kim, Jared Brown-Rabinowitz, Harriette "Meema" McCullers Brinkley, Ciro Lopez, Gloria Fortune, Linda Chupkowski, Chloe Palenchar, Zorian Palenkowski, Artem Palenkowski, Kaveh Akbar, Paige Lewis, Dean Bakopoulos (my brother), Melissa Febos, Donika Kelly, Matthew Olzmann, Vievee Francis, Alex Chee, Dustin Schnell, Fran Offenhauser, Michael Mekeel, Mikie Mekeel, Niki Sri-Kumar, Nara and Reya, Sandra Lim, Tracy K. Smith, Sally Keith, Jennifer Grotz, Danielle Purifoy, Antonia Randolph, Jennifer Ho, Matthew Grady, Destiny Hemphill, Sarah Long, Kelly Alexander, Sharon Holland, Jaki Shelton Green, Gabriel Bump, Lauren Christensen, Simone (Miss You), Noah, Tonia Poteat, Bhargav Adagarla, Tom Coombs, Andrea Knittel, Lynn Eckert, Jenny Lind, Erin Zimring, Daniel Pipski, my whole beautiful cohort at the Harvard Radcliffe Institute and everyone who made my life so great there, William Cheng, Maxine Gordon, Tawanna Dillahunt, Isabel Galleymore, Daniel Wallace, Laura Wallace, Stephanie Elizondo Griest, Melissa Faliveno, Carlina Duan, Karen Tucker, Jared Lipof, Matt Randal O'Wain, Mesha Maren, Adam Price, Ross White, Julia Ridley Smith, Bland Simpson, Michael Gutierrez, Joe Fletcher, Kylan Rice, Mary Floyd-Wilson, Eliza Richards, Meta DuEwa Jones, Angela Valez, Jennifer Washington, Marsha Collins, Emily Wallace,

Ayşe Erginer, my whole UNC Chapel Hill family, Alexa Dilworth, Michael Parker, Ippy Patterson, Ellen Cassilly, Frank Kornhaus, Meg Day, Chelsea Reimann, Mathias Svalina, Airea D. Matthews, Coco Wilder, Alta Feddeman, Gabriel Fried and the Persea Family, Heidi and Jeff and everyone at Bluestem Conservation Cemetery, Tiana Clark, Marlanda Dekine, Debra Allbery and everyone at Warren Wilson Program for Writers, all the poets who live lives of love and radical action that inspire me, my students who teach me, my teachers near and far, Mark Doty, Paula Mauro, Ann Cadigan, Brian Teare, Amy G. Lehman, Max Lehman, Michele Rugani, David Adjmi, Everyone who's shown me such care and kindness.

I apologize to anyone whose name I've forgotten in this moment. I am grateful to you. I will remember.

For those practitioners whose expertise and compassion took me through and continue to: Darius Russell, Terencia Russell, Joyce, Mike, and everyone at Russell's Pharmacy (Miss You) in Old East Durham. Pierre and Robin Dubois. Melinda P. Everett, Pat Chapell, Katherine Rowe, Chris Helmstetter, and Joe Gilbert.

To the editors, magazines, and journals that featured these poems. Thank you. Poems from this manuscript have appeared in some form in: Academy of American Poets Poem-a-Day, *The American Poetry Review, The Baffler, The Nation, The New Yorker, Orion, Oxford American, Poetry,* and *Tin House.*

To Kimberly Witherspoon and everyone at Inkwell Management. I owe you so much and I appreciate you beyond words.

For the extraordinary team at Copper Canyon. Thank you for this new chapter. Michael Wiegers, Ryo Yamaguchi, Ashley E. Wynter, Claretta Holsey, David Caligiuri, Rowan Sharp, the remarkable interns. You are incredible. I appreciate you.

For my family: Tom Calvocoressi, Lisa Calvocoressi, Remarkable Sibling Ameya Calvocoressi, Serendipling Rousz DeLuca, Valerie Tourais Harris, Martha Shethar, Eric Shethar, Yoshi Shaka, Helina Shaka, Joe Guardiola.

Eavan Boland. Miss You. Richard Howard. Miss You. Lucie Brock-Broido. Miss You.

Paul Otremba. Miss You. Jenny Tone-Pah-Hote. Miss You. Randall Kenan. Miss You.

For the animals who tended me and taught me as I wrote this book. Daisy (Miss You), Greta, GEORGE, Inky (Miss You), Clemente (Miss You), Kekoa (Miss You), Kawena Batou.

For the friends who read this book, kept reading this book, kept rooting me on, kept asking questions, kept loving me and my poems: Jonathan Farmer, Tyree Daye, Vaughan Ashlie Fielder, Nikky Finney, and Dana Levin. You save my life. This book is for you.

Oliver Leek, Tim Leek, and Jill Lepore offered me a room in their house while I was at Radcliffe. It became a home and friend-family I could never have imagined. Rachel F. Seidman made it so. Thank you. There's no book without you.

Each night I open my heart and mind as far as it can go. I imagine every being I've met and everyone I haven't. I name everyone I can and I try and open the portal. I say into the darkness:

May we be happy, may we be healthy, may we be free from suffering, may we be full of joy.

May we be free from COVID-19 and cancer and all forms of illness.

May we be free from all forms of anxiety and all desperation.

May we be free from all forms of gun violence.

May we be loved, honored, sheltered, and held.

Angeline Shaka, you are my hope and my homecoming.
You are the deepest prayer answered every day.

About the Author

Gabrielle Calvocoressi is the author of *The Last Time I Saw Amelia Earhart, Apocalyptic Swing* (a finalist for the LA Times Book Prize), and *Rocket Fantastic,* winner of the Audre Lorde Award for Lesbian Poetry. Calvocoressi was the Beatrice Shepherd Blane Fellow at the Harvard-Radcliffe Institute for 2022–2023. They are also the recipient of other awards and fellowships, including a Stegner Fellowship and Jones Lectureship from Stanford University; a Rona Jaffe Woman Writer's Award; a Lannan Foundation residency in Marfa, Texas; the Bernard F. Conners Prize from *The Paris Review;* and a residency from the Civitella di Ranieri Foundation. Calvocoressi's poems have been published or are forthcoming in numerous magazines and journals, including *The American Poetry Review, The Baffler, Boston Review, Kenyon Review, The Nation, The New Yorker, The New York Times, Poetry,* and *Tin House.* Calvocoressi is an editor at large at *The Los Angeles Review of Books* and poetry editor at *Southern Cultures.* Calvocoressi teaches at UNC-Chapel Hill and lives in Old East Durham, North Carolina, where joy, compassion, and social justice are at the center of their personal and poetic practice.

POETS FOR POETRY

Copper Canyon Press poets are at the center of all our efforts as a nonprofit publisher. Poets create the art of our books, and they read and teach the books we publish. Many are also generous donors who believe in financially supporting the vibrant poetry community of Copper Canyon Press. For decades, our poets have quietly donated their royalties, have contributed their time to our fundraising campaigns, and have made personal donations in support of emerging and established poets. Their generosity has encouraged the innovative risk-taking that sustains and furthers the art form.

The donor-poets who have contributed to the Press since 2023 include:

Jonathan Aaron
Pamela Alexander
Kazim Ali
Ellen Bass
Erin Belieu
Mark Bibbins
Linda Bierds
Sherwin Bitsui
Jaswinder Bolina
Marianne Boruch
Laure-Anne Bosselaar
Cyrus Cassells
Peter Cole and Adina Hoffman
Elizabeth J. Coleman
Shangyang Fang
John Freeman
Forrest Gander
Jenny George
Dan Gerber
Jorie Graham
Roger Greenwald
Robert and Carolyn Hedin
Bob Hicok
Ha Jin
The estate of Jaan Kaplinski
Laura Kasischke
Jennifer L. Knox
Ted Kooser
Stephen Kuusisto
Deborah Landau
Sung-Il Lee
Ben Lerner
Dana Levin
Maurice Manning
Heather McHugh
Jane Miller
Roger Mitchell
Lisa Olstein
Gregory Orr
Eric Pankey
Kevin Prufer
Alicia Rabins
Dean Rader
Paisley Rekdal
James Richardson
Alberto Ríos
David Romtvedt
Sarah Ruhl
Kelli Russell Agodon
Natalie Shapero
Arthur Sze
Yuki Tanaka
Elaine Terranova
Chase Twichell
Ocean Vuong
Connie Wanek
Emily Warn

Poetry is vital to language and living. Since 1972, Copper Canyon Press has published extraordinary poetry from around the world to engage the imaginations and intellects of readers, writers, booksellers, librarians, teachers, students, and donors.

We are grateful for the major support provided by:

academy of american poets

OFFICE OF ARTS & CULTURE

SEATTLE

The Witter Bynner Foundation for Poetry

TO LEARN MORE ABOUT UNDERWRITING COPPER CANYON PRESS TITLES, PLEASE CALL 360-385-4925 EXT. 105

We are grateful for the major support provided by:

Anonymous

Jill Baker and Jeffrey Bishop

Anne and Geoffrey Barker

Mona Baroudi and Patrick Whitgrove

Lisha Bian

Rick Shinsui Bowles

John Branch

Diana Broze

John R. Cahill

Sarah J. Cavanaugh

Keith Cowan and Linda Walsh

Peter Currie

Geralyn White Dreyfous

The Evans Family

Mimi Gardner Gates

Claire Gribbin

Gull Industries Inc. on behalf of William True

Carolyn and Robert Hedin

David and Jane Hibbard

Bruce S. Kahn

Phil Kovacevich and Eric Wechsler

Eric La Brecque

Maureen Lee and Mark Busto

Ellie Mathews and Carl Youngmann as The North Press

Kathryn O'Driscoll

Petunia Charitable Fund and advisor Elizabeth Hebert

Suzanne Rapp and Mark Hamilton

Adam and Lynn Rauch

Emily and Dan Raymond

Joseph C. Roberts

Cynthia Sears

Kim and Jeff Seely

Tree Swenson

Julia Sze

Donna Wolf

Jamie Wolf

Barbara and Charles Wright

In honor of C.D. Wright from Forrest Gander

Caleb Young as C. Young Creative

The dedicated interns and faithful volunteers of Copper Canyon Press

The pressmark for Copper Canyon Press
suggests entrance, connection, and interaction
while holding at its center
an attentive, dynamic space for poetry.

This book is set in Arno Pro.
Book design by Phil Kovacevich.
Printed on archival-quality paper.